Inspired by a Garden

Poems by Marilyn Kratz

Paintings by Beverly Behrens

For my friend Elaine —

Marilyn Kratz

July 3, 2022

ISBN 978-1-7923-7842-3

Cover illustration, mixed flowers, by Beverly Behrens
Cover Design by Ralph Behrens

First printing October 2021

Published by: Prairie Hearth Publishing, LLC
Yankton, South Dakota

Dedications

I dedicate this book to the fond memories of my dear Mother, Aunt Effie, and their country gardens. As I recall their plantings, from friendly springtime pansies to elegant autumnal mums, I am inspired. Those displays are now reflected in my front yard flowers and my spare-of-space patio — and they often find new life among my watercolors.

BB

I dedicate this book to all who love gardens with the hope that it inspires that love in everyone else who reads it. It is also my way of presenting a huge bouquet of thankfulness for many happy hours spent in my gardens over the years and for the support I have from my husband Bud, even when I ask him to snap a pail full of green beans or dice dozens of rhubarb stalks.

MK

Table of Contents

Introduction   1
    Farm House on Brick Church Road, Walworth, WI (painting)   2
    When to Write a Poem (poem)   3

Spring   4
    Dutch Iris (painting)   5
    Crocus (painting)   6
    Spring at Last (poem)   7
    Melody Farm Nature Preserve, Lake Forest, IL (painting)   8
    It's Too Late Now – Hooray! (poem)   9
    Rhubarb (painting)   10
    Rhubarb Rollick (poem)   11
    Daffodils (painting)   12
    The First Time You Saw Daffodils (poem)   13
    Pansy Pitcher (painting)   14
    Pansies (poem)   15

Summer   16
    Zinnias (painting)   17
    Grandma's Roses (painting)   18
    Good Question (poem)   19
    House on Vine, Lake Forest, IL (painting)   20
    How to Cool a Hot Summer Day (poem)   21
    The Humming Bird's Visit (painting)   22
    Humbled in My Garden (poem)   23
    Egg Plant, Tomatoes, and Green Pepper (painting)   24
    This Morning, I Tasted Warm Summer Sunshine (poem)   25
    Rose (painting)   26
    Last Roses of Summer (poem)   27

Fall 28

    White Oak (painting) 29

    Staghorn Sumac (painting) 30

    Autumn Lullaby (poem) 31

    Chrysanthemum Garden (painting) 32

    Autumn Scent (poem) 33

    Sunflower (painting) 34

    Faded Beauty (poem) 35

    Native Wildflowers (painting) 36

    Weeds (poem) 37

    Autumn Still Life (painting) 38

    Inspired by My Apple Tree (poem) 39

Winter 40

    Poinsettia (painting) 41

    Garden's Winter Scene (painting) 42

    Frost Descending (poem) 43

    Geranium Niche (painting) 44

    Summer on My Window Sill (poem) 45

    Farm on Six Corners Road, Walworth Couny, WI (painting) 46

    Hunkering Down (poem) 47

    Delphiniums and Zinnias (painting) 48

    The Gardener's Reward (poem) 49

    Beyond the Winter (painting) 50

    February Thaw (poem) 51

    Zucchini Blossom (painting) 52

    Ode to a Zucchini Blossom (poem) 53

Acknowledgements 54

Introduction

Farm House on Brick Church Road,

Walworth County, WI

When to Write a Poem

When the aroma of bread baking in your oven brings back memories of Mama,
    A kitten warms your lap and soothes away your worries with its velvety purr,
    Your spouse says, "I love you," every day after more than sixty years together,
    Or you welcome your children and grandchildren home for a Christmas visit;

When the first crocus pops out of a patch of dirty snow and promises winter will soon end,
    You pick the first green beans of the season from your garden,
    A butterfly flits from flower to flower beside you and doesn't care that you're there,
    Or autumn leaves reflect the blaze of blooming mums along the fence;

When a double rainbow arches across the sky after a refreshing summer rainstorm,
    Prairie grasses ripple in waves as a lusty wind sings its wild song,
    Pheasants soar over fields of tawny cornstalks under brilliant blue October skies,
    Or the setting sun splashes the sky with neon colors no artist could imagine;

When the promise of a new adventure arouses that excited little flutter inside you,
    Life bestows gifts upon you in full measure when you aren't expecting them,
    You feel the satisfaction of a job well done,
    Or you pull the blanket to your chin after a long day and sink your head into the pillow;

How can you not write a poem?

Spring

Dutch Iris, *Iris holliandica*

Crocus

Spring at Last

Just when it seems we can't abide

Another day of cold and snow,

Bleak winter clouds dissolve in rain,

And winter's grime begins to go.

Now grass takes on a fresh green hue;

A robin checks out last year's nest.

The lilac bushes, kissed by sun,

Unfurl their leaves and look well-dressed.

And then, to crown the season's start,

And reassure us it will stay,

A patch of eager crocuses

Lifts up its soft pastel display.

Melody Farm Nature Preserve,

Lake Forest, IL

It's Too Late Now - Hooray!

It'll have to wait – it's too late now.

I've something more important to do than
> Check expiration dates on pills
>> Or strip the wax from floors
>>> Or decide what to take to the church potluck.

A welcome summons wafts through a window –
> The smell of earth, damp and expectant,
>> The breeze, slightly balmy instead of icy,
>>> Tulips peeking out to be sure they have their timing
>>> right.

It's finally here, and now it's too late for inside jobs.
> I must be out, touching silk petals of crocuses,
>> Checking to see what survived winter,
>>> Deciding where to plant those new roses.

It's time now for the busyness of Spring. Hurray!

Rhubarb, Rheum x hybridum

Rhubarb Rollick

The surest sign that spring's around
Is rhubarb peeking through the ground.
It starts with leaves so crinkly green;
Before you blink, tall stalks are seen.

Then comes the sauce, some jam, a cake,
And lots of rhubarb pies to bake,
And rhubarb muffins, rhubarb tarts –
Whoa! Rhubarb glaze on chicken parts?

Soon comes the time when you must say,
"Let's give this last rhubarb away!
It's starting now to sicken us.
We're ready for asparagus!"

Daffodils

The First Time You Saw Daffodils

Though you've grown into an accomplished adult now,

I still remember when I first held you in my arms.

I marveled at what a miniature miracle you were.

You closed your baby eyes and pursed your mouth into a 'leave me alone'

pout.

I curled your wee hand around my thumb

And gazed at your fingernails – no bigger than a wren's eyes.

Your aunt came to see you and said, "She's so little!"

I insisted, "She's just the right size."

I dressed you in ruffles and lace and dresses I sewed to match mine.

You changed so fast it almost took my breath away.

I wanted each moment - each change - to last long enough

To etch a permanent picture in my memory.

At first, your dependence upon me

Filled my heart with a mellow mixture of pride and fear.

Then your world expanded, and I had to share you

With picture books, Grandma and Grandpa, and a spoon you could hold

yourself.

One day, in your second spring, I suddenly realized

You had given me the priceless gift of seeing the world anew.

It happened when I saw the dazzle in your eyes

The first time you saw daffodils.

Pansy Pitcher

Pansies

At Spring's first touch of warmth,
They burst through last year's turf,
Unfurling soft green leaves
And breaking forth in bloom.

With jaunty faces to the sun,
Purple, yellow, pink, and white,
They flirt with lilting breezes,
And dance to songs of robins.

Of all the joys of spring
Inspiring prayers of thanks,
None surpass the beauty
Of pansies' smiling faces.

Summer

Zinnias

Grandma's Roses

Good Question

What are you doing, Grandma?

Weeding my flower garden.

Why?

So my flowers have room to grow.

What's your favorite flower, Grandma?

Now let me think. I guess I like roses best.

Which color is your favorite, Grandma?

Yellow, definitely yellow. I love all yellow flowers.

Then why did you pull out that yellow dandelion, Grandma?

House on Vine, Lake Forest, IL

How to Cool a Hot Summer Day

Wind scours the meadow, bending thistles down

And whipping grass into rippling waves.

The sun seems to stall over towns at noon, scorching lawns,

Baking asphalt streets, hurrying shoppers from awing to awning

Till they escape into air-conditioned stores.

Even avid gardeners abandon their bean patches,

Forced indoors behind drawn drapes by unrelenting heat.

Roses not picked early in the morning wilt on canes,

Bowing their heads in dejected defeat.

A dog sits on the north side of the garage,

Tongue hanging out as he pants away his misery.

Farmers peer out of barn doors,

Searching the sky for rain clouds and courage.

By mid-afternoon, everyone is ready to call it a day.

It's too hot to work, too hot to play.

All that's left to do is eat ice-cold watermelon

And hope the hot spell doesn't last much longer.

The Hummingbird's Visit

Humbled in My Garden

To ants, scurrying away from my clumping boots,
I am a giant, foreign and fearful.

Butterflies sipping nectar as I approach zinnias
Float off when I reach to cut stems of orange-sherbet blossoms.

Even hungry rabbits scamper off when I approach,
Afraid to linger despite two bean plants left to demolish.

A bumblebee, fat and fuzzy, zips away from the crimson rose
When I stop to sniff its delicate scent.

I am taller than the cana plant beside me,
Even though it's the tallest plant in my garden.

Surely, I am ruler of my garden kingdom,
The one most respected and revered by visiting critters.

Then a hummingbird whirs just six inches from my face,
Refusing to fear me while enjoying her sugary cana breakfast,

And I gladly relinquish my crown to her.

Egg Plant, Tomatoes, and Green Pepper

Solanum melongena, Solanum lycopersicum, Capsicum annum

This Morning, I Tasted Warm Summer Sunshine

...in the form the first ripe cherry tomato from my garden.
There it was – red and firm and glowing,
An invitation to a tiny but long anticipated feast.
I popped it into my mouth and crunched it,
The warm, sweet juice flowing over my tongue
Like a burst of blessing from nature itself.
Soon I'll pick buckets full of these treasures,
Sometimes plucking them from vines
Before they have completed their transformation
From promising orange to irresistible red.
They'll sit in a basket on my kitchen counter,
Taking their time to finish ripening safely indoors,
Washed and ready for me to snitch one
Every time I walk anywhere near that bounty.
I'll enjoy every one, but none so much
As the first one of summer
I savored right there in my garden today.

Rose

Last Roses of Summer

I cut an armful of rose buds

To rescue from frost's first bite.

The petals curl tightly atop willowy stems,

Unable to unfurl on days too short to warm their hearts.

After a day or two luxuriating

In a vase on my dining room table,

They timidly uncurl a petal here and there

And decide to risk one last showing.

A yellow rose opens into a blaze of silky sunshine.

A clump of brilliant orange buds become a neon cluster.

Two apricot-tinted blossom compete to see

Which can unfurl the most petals

And become the biggest blossom

Taken from the bush all summer.

A rose-pink bud opens with a creamy throat

To dispense a fragrance so intoxicating

That it attracts fruit flies.

I sit at my table and enjoy one last gift of summer,

And I dream of next spring's roses.

Fall

White Oak, *Quercus alba*

Staghorn Sumac, *Rhus hirta*

Autumn Lullaby

The frantic pace of summer gardening ebbs

As days grow shorter and nights turn cooler.

Green tomatoes hang from tired, drooping vines,

Waiting for me pluck and store them to ripen inside.

Dry leaves from beanstalks crackle underfoot,

As I yank stubborn tendrils from wire support cages.

Roses are mulched, gladiola corms dug.

Only hearty mums match the brilliant colors

Of leaves drifting down from trees.

No more hectic days of canning and freezing;

No more weeds to pull or rows to hoe.

The garden is ready to rest under snowy blankets

And listen to the song of northern winds overhead.

Winter waits to bring its welcome reprieve

From days of toil under hot, summer sun.

I walk away from the dying garden,

Ready to listen for my own winter lullaby,

As comforting as my rocker's squeak,

And smile, for to me, winter wind heralds spring

When I'll be happy to start all the work again.

Chrysanthemum Garden

Autumn Scent

A blaze of blooming mums brightens the corner of my garden,

Giving off a heady fragrance that speaks of autumn

While offering up memories of spring and summer past.

I inhale their pungent perfume and find hints of

The intense temptations of basil and oregano

And the tang of ripe tomatoes glowing red in sultry sun.

Then the aroma brings me back to this season,

And I appreciate mustiness of fallen leaves in cold rain,

Nostalgic wafts of smoky bonfires on chill evening breezes,

And candles singeing the insides of Jack-o-lanterns.

All are combined in that spicy mum scent

That speaks of autumn as nothing else can.

It has a note of finality, and yet it excites me,

For beyond its prediction of winter's cold and snow,

It promises another spring and summer to follow,

Reflected in sturdy petals as I inhale the unique fragrance

Of blazing mums decorating a corner in my garden.

Sunflower, *Helianthus annuus*

Faded Beauty

(Haiku)

Limp, faded petals

Drift down and leave behind them

Promises in seeds.

Native Wildflowers

Weeds

Optimism sprouts in early spring

When the garden is still just a plan

Waiting to come to life on bare ground.

Possibilities loom, fruitful, abundant, and weed free.

Enthusiasm continues into early summer

When plants start to show promise

Of abundant harvests to come,

And it feels important to pull weeds.

Late summer days are busy, picking and preserving,

And weeds are noticed only if they have shot up

Near enough to cucumber or tomato plants

To make them convenient to pull.

The first frost reduces the bulk of plant refuse

By wilting leaves and killing everything green.

Then it's a pleasure to plan next year's garden

Without a single thought to pulling weeds.

Autumn Still Life

Inspired by My Apple Tree

It welcomes spring with silky blossoms,

Like fluffy clouds trapped in the branches.

Soon petals float down to kiss the grass

Before disappearing in minute tufts of brown.

Leaves unfurl as tiny apples begin to grow

Where happy bees had visited to collect pollen.

As summer warms to its climax,

The apples grow, green and hard and shiny.

Then early autumn paints streaks of red along their cheeks.

When the last remnants of green around the stem

Fade into warm yellow, they are ready.

They signal their willingness to share the crop

By dropping – plop, plop, plop – around the tree.

I hasten to pick those, perfect and unbruised, still on the branches.

All winter long, I feast on apple sauce, apple pies, apple crisp,

Already dreaming of next year's crop.

How could I not write a poem about such extravagant pleasure?

Winter

Poinsettia, *Euphorbia pulcherrima*

Garden's Winter Scene

Frost Descending

I glance out the window at my garden immobilized by merciless
cold

Despite brittle sunshine casting blue shadows across the snow.

Trees, naked after fall leaf drop, hunker under coats of bristly frost.

White, white, white blankets all I can see.

Then the first breeze of day awakes.

It shakes dormant trees and sleeping rose canes,

And frost floats down soundlessly,

Each separate spike unique and grand.

First, just a few brave shards glint in morning's light.

Then more shake loose,

And the air is filled with tiny dancing sparkles –

An imitation snowfall –

Creating beauty so intense it overwhelms the icy air,

And my garden shimmers in delight.

Geranium Niche

Summer on My Windowsill

Outside the grass is dormant brown

With crusty dabs of dirty snow.

The trees stand naked, bending back,

While 'round them winter's cold winds blow.

I gaze out at the chill March world

Beyond my frosty windowpane

And wish for summer's bright warm days,

A wish I know I make in vain.

Then, looking down I see a sight

That gives my heart a warm spring thrill.

Geraniums have blossomed red –

It's summer on my windowsill!

Farm on Six Corners Road,

Walworth County, WI

Hunkering Down

Trees curl their toes under a blanket of soggy leaves

While lawns, still green, slow down their growth

And anticipate the on-coming dormant time.

Rose bushes gratefully accept an extra mound of soil

Snuggled around their roots by the attentive gardener.

Squirrels lay in a winter's supply of seeds and acorns

And add more dry grass inside their tree homes.

Songbirds bid good-bye to summer roosts and head south,

Rushing to avoid harsh winds and deep snow.

Houseplants that had enjoyed a summer vacation on the porch

Are content to be inside, resting on a shelf

And basking in sunshine pouring in through windowpanes.

Gardeners pack away straw hats and soil-stained shirts and jeans

And air out sweaters, coats, and scarves.

Winter is coming with icy mornings and frigid nights,

But all is well as the world tightens up, hunkers down,

And prepares to weather long, cold days while dreaming of spring.

Delphiniums and Zinnias

The Gardener's Reward

This day in March it starts because I found
Three little deep purple crocuses
Poking up on the south side of the house,
Defying snow still crusted around them
And winter wind that bites my fingers.
I pinch them off as far down the stem as possible
And arrange them in a tiny vase,
The first of many beautiful bouquets
I'll enjoy during gardening season.

Next will come tulips and daffodils,
Adding splashes of primary colors to my yard,
Still clothed in winter browns.
Before they fade, peonies will burst open,
So heavy with perfumed petals that they droop
Over the bushy plants, making a feathery pink and purple hedge.
Yellow-hearted white daisies will bloom just in time
For me to include their bright faces in bouquets
Of jaunty columbines and elegant irises.

A patch of coreopsis, self-planted from last year's seeds,
Shows off blossoms of mini golden suns
Just as climbing roses begin blanketing the trellis
With clusters of fragrant, deep pink blossoms,
Soon joined by multi-colored tea roses, queens of the garden.
All summer, gladiolas, zinnias, petunias, and snap dragons
Will provide flowers to keep me supplied,
Reminding me, on this cold winter day,
That every time I arrange a new bouquet,
I have been paid for enduring winter's frosty cold
And summer's diligent weeding, watering, and hoeing.

Beyond the Winter

February Thaw

Frigid winds whip through the yard
Leaving banks of snow behind,
But I don't feel cruel winter's chill;
I have warmer scenes in mind.

I see banks of daffodils,
Tulips splash their colors bright.
Daisies nod beside pink phlox,
Roses share their sweet delight.

Lush green lettuce forms crisp heads,
Green beans flourish, fresh dill grows.
Squash plants blossom right beside
Kale and chard in long straight rows.

Not a sign of weed or wilt
Steals my gardening joy away.
Inspiration is at hand -
New seed catalogs came today!

Zucchini Blossom

Ode to a Zucchini Blossom

(And finally, what is a garden without zucchini plants, big and glorious,
producing abundant fruits for you to share?)

From the day I planted seeds in spring-warmed earth
Until timid sprouts bravely poked out their first leaves,
I watched and worried about my garden,
Source of summer happiness and succulent produce.
Will rain come at the right time?
Has it been too cool at night for the beans?
Is that an insect hole in a cucumber plant leaf?
When was the last time I saw a bee around here
To pollinate blossoms when they open?
Then, one late spring day, I see through the window
A big, bright, yellow spot amidst the garden's green.
I hurry out to check, and there it is in all its glory –
A zucchini blossom, bigger than my hand,
Gleaming up at the sun.
At last, I have a promise of things to come,
And I wonder why I worried so.

Acknowledgements

I am grateful to the following publications in which the poems listed were previously published, sometimes in slightly different forms:

Pasque Petals, Spring 2009 - "Spring, At Last"

Pasque Petals, Spring 2009 - "Too Late Now – Hurray!"

Pasque Petals, Spring 2004 - "The First Time You Saw Daffodils"

Pasque Petals, Spring 2020 - "Humbled in My Garden"

Yankton County Observer, April 30, 2021, "Rhubarb Rollick"

Pasque Petals, Fall 2011; Yankton County Observer, September 2020 - "The Last Roses of Summer"

Pasque Petals, Fall 2018 - "Autumn Scent"

Pasque Petals, Summer 2006 - "Faded Beauty"

South Dakota Magazine, Nov./Dec. 2012 - "Frost Descending"

South Dakota Magazine, Mar./Apr. 2005 – "Summer on My Windowsill"